Althea Gibson
Terry Barber

Sports Series

Text copyright © 2007 Terry Barber

Photographs copyright © in the names of individual photographers, artists, and organizations as noted specifically on page 51.

All rights reserved. No part of this book may be reproduced or transmitted in any form or by an means, including photocopy, recording, or any information storage and retrieval system, without the prior written permission of the publisher.

Althea Gibson is published by
Grass Roots Press, a division of Literacy Services of Canada Ltd.

www.grassrootsbooks.net

ACKNOWLEDGMENTS

We acknowledge the financial support of the Government of Canada through the Canada Book Fund (CBF) for our publishing activities.

Produced with the assistance of the Government of Alberta, Alberta Multimedia Development Fund.

Editor: Dr. Pat Campbell
Image research: Dr. Pat Campbell
Book design: Lara Minja, Lime Design Inc.

Library and Archives Canada Cataloguing in Publication

Barber, Terry, date
    Althea Gibson / Althea Gibson.

ISBN 978-1-894593-59-5

    1. Gibson, Althea, 1927–2003. 2. African American women tennis players—Biography. 3. Tennis players—United States—Biography. 4. Readers for new literates. I. Title.

PE1126.N43B3648 2007   428.6'2   C2007-902779-2

Contents

A Star is Born..5
The Great Depression..7
Growing up in Harlem.......................................11
Althea Learns Tennis...23
Althea Becomes Famous...................................29
The Queen of Tennis...37
A Trailblazer..43
Glossary..47
Talking About the Book....................................49

These farmers pick cotton.

A Star is Born

It is 1927. A baby girl is born. She is born on a cotton farm. Her name is Althea Gibson. Althea will become the first black tennis star.

> Althea is born in Silver, South Carolina.

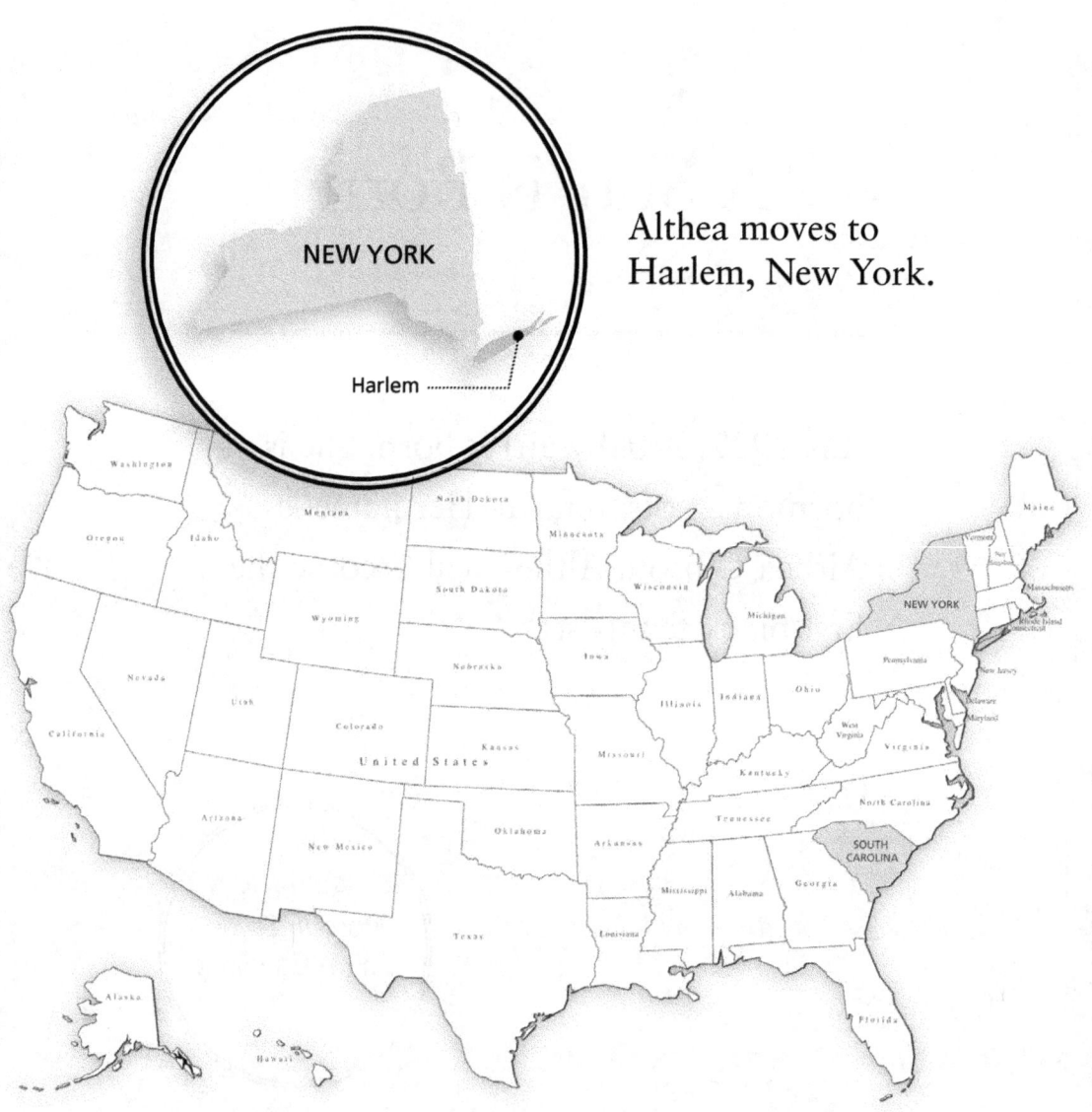

Althea moves to Harlem, New York.

The Great Depression

Althea's parents work on a cotton farm. They are very poor. Althea's father makes $75 a year.

In the 1930s, many black people move to Harlem. They want a better life. When Althea is three, she moves to Harlem with her family.

> In 1930, about 34,000 cotton farmers move to Harlem.

These men do not have jobs. They eat at a soup kitchen.

The Great Depression

The **Great Depression** takes place in the 1930s. The world is a hard place. Jobs are hard to find. Many people cannot pay their rent. Many people do not have a roof over their head. People cannot buy food.

The Depression lasts from 1929 to 1939.

These men beg for work.

An apartment in Harlem.

Growing up in Harlem

Althea is a young girl in the 1930s. Althea is lucky. Her parents have jobs. Her family lives in a small apartment. Althea has food on her plate. She has a roof over her head.

In 1932, about 13 million Americans cannot find jobs.

People play music.

Growing up in Harlem

Althea grows up in Harlem. Many black people call Harlem home. The streets are alive with people. Children play on the streets. People play music on the streets. People sell food on the streets.

These boys play stickball.

Growing up in Harlem

Althea is good at sports. She plays ball on the streets. She plays basketball. She plays **stickball**. She does it all so well. She is really good at paddle tennis. Althea has so much energy.

Althea is a paddle tennis champ between 1938 to 1942.

Children read in a Harlem school.

Growing up in Harlem

In fact, Althea has too much energy. She would rather have a ball in her hand than a book. Althea stays away from school for days at a time. Althea gets into trouble for not going to school.

The Society for the Prevention of Cruelty to Children

Growing up in Harlem

Althea lives by her own rules. Her parents cannot control her. Her father beats her for not going to school. Her father beats her for coming home late. Sometimes, Althea runs away. She goes to a place that protects children.

Althea goes to the Society for the Prevention of Cruelty to Children.

A movie theatre.

Growing up in Harlem

Althea also loves movies. She **skips** school to see movies. The movie does not even have to be good. Sports and movies. Althea skips school to do both.

Fred Johnson in 2003.
He plays tennis with one arm.

Althea Learns Tennis

Althea starts to play tennis. She has the best coach in Harlem. His name is Fred Johnson.

Althea's first tennis lesson is in 1941. Fred teaches Althea to learn from her mistakes. Fred thinks that Althea will become great.

2.5 million black men serve in World War II.

Althea Learns Tennis

Althea plays tennis during World War II. The war lasts from 1939 to 1945. Althea wins her first ATA tennis game in 1942.

> The ATA stands for American Tennis Association. Black people form the ATA in 1916.

Althea trains hard.

Althea Learns Tennis

It is 1946. Althea meets another man named Johnson. Dr. Walter Johnson watches Althea play tennis. Althea loses in the finals. To Dr. Johnson, Althea's loss does not matter. Dr. Johnson sees how great Althea can become.

Dr. Johnson supports Althea's training. She works hard. Her tennis gets better. She wins many ATA tennis games.

These women **protest** segregation.

Althea Becomes Famous

The sport of tennis is **segregated**.
Black people play tennis with blacks.
White people play with whites.
Dr. Johnson thinks Althea can break
the colour **barrier**. He thinks she has
the key to unlock the door.

Althea walks to the tennis court at Forest Hills.

Althea Becomes Famous

The best tennis in the U.S. is played at Forest Hills. It is the home of the U.S. Open tennis championship. Black people cannot play in the U.S. Open.

In 1950, the rules change. Althea can play in the U.S. Open. She does not win. But she changes history.

> At age 23, Althea breaks the colour barrier.

Althea shakes hands after a match.

Althea Becomes Famous

Tennis players are good sports. They shake hands after a match. The players may say, "Good match." Sometimes, Althea is not a good sport. She may say nothing. Or she may say, "I'll get you next time." Althea plays to win.

Althea's smile can fill a room.

Althea Becomes Famous

Althea's tennis game gets better and better. Tennis fans know her name. Althea's face is in the newspapers. People like her. Althea's smile can fill a room. People want to see her play tennis.

Althea gets her university degree in 1953.

Althea plays at Wimbledon, England.

The Queen of Tennis

In 1957, Althea goes to England. She plays at Wimbledon. She plays the best tennis players in the world. She wins the singles title. Althea is the first black person to win the title. Althea is the queen of tennis.

Althea sits with her proud parents,
Annie and Daniel Gibson.

The Queen of Tennis

Althea returns home. She is a hero. There is a parade in her honour. Althea's family is so proud. Althea's father says, "This is the proudest day of my life."

New York City gives Althea a parade.

Althea wins the U.S. Open on September 9, 1957.

The Queen of Tennis

In 1957, Althea plays at Forest Hills. This time, she wins the U.S. Open. She is the first black person to win the U.S. Open. Althea is named Female Athlete of the Year.

In 1958, Althea wins her second U.S. Open.

Althea plays at the U.S. Open.

Althea's book is published in 1958.

A Trailblazer

Althea retires from tennis. She writes a book about her life. It is called *I Always Wanted to Be Somebody*. Althea has become somebody. She has become a great tennis player. She has broken the colour barrier.

Serena Williams wins the U.S. Open in 1999. She is the first African American woman to win since Althea Gibson. Serena (left) and Venus (right) Williams.

The Williams sisters say, "Althea Gibson paved the way for us."

A Trailblazer

Althea Gibson dies in September 2003. Althea was a **trailblazer**. Althea left a path for others to follow. Today, it is a well-worn path. We must not forget that Althea set this path.

Althea supports inner city children who want to play tennis.

Glossary

barrier: something that blocks the way.

Great Depression: a time of high unemployment, falling prices, and low wages.

protest: to complain about something.

segregate: to separate a race or class from the rest of society.

skip: not attend.

stickball: a form of baseball that uses a rubber ball and a broomstick.

trailblazer: a person who leads the way.

Talking About the Book

What did you learn about Althea Gibson?

What words would you use to describe Althea?

What challenges did Althea face in her life?

Althea broke the colour barrier. What do you think this means?

The Williams sisters say, "Althea Gibson paved the way for us." What do you think this means?

Why does the author call Althea a trailblazer?

Picture Credits

Front cover photos (center photo): © Bettman/Corbis. (small photo): © Bettmann/CORBIS. **Contents page** (top left): © AP. (bottom left): © Library of Congress, Prints and Photographs Division, LC-USZ62-118872. (bottom right): © AP. **Page 4:** © Library of Congress, Prints and Photographs Division, LC-USZ62-94029. **Page 7:** © Library of Congress, Prints and Photographs Division, LC-USF34-056099-D. **Page 8:** © Library of Congress, Prints and Photographs Division, LC-USZ62-47866. **Page 9:** © Library of Congress, Prints and Photographs Division, LC-USZ62-122459. **Page 10:** © Library of Congress, Prints and Photographs Division, LC-USW3-024048-E. **Page 12:** © Library of Congress, Prints and Photographs Division, LC-USW3-031109-C. **Page 13:** © Library of Congress, Prints and Photographs Division, LC-USW3-023989-E. **Page 14:** © Lucien Aigner/CORBIS. **Page 16:** © Lucien Aigner/CORBIS. **Page 18:** © The George Sim Johnston Archives of The New York Society for the Prevention of Cruelty to Children. **Page 20:** © Library of Congress, Prints and Photographs Division, LC-USF342-T01-001285-A. **Page 21:** © Library of Congress, Prints and Photographs Division, LC-USF33-T01-001086-M3. **Page 22:** © Time Life Pictures/Getty Images. **Page 24:** © National Archives, 208-NP-4HHH-2. **Page 26:** © AP. **Page 28:** © Library of Congress, Prints and Photographs Division, LC-USZ62-118872. **Page 30:** © Library of Congress, Prints and Photographs Division, LC-USZ62-115926. **Page 32:** © Bettmann/CORBIS. **Page 34:** © Bettman/Corbis. **Page 36:** © Library of Congress, Prints and Photographs Division, LC-USZ62-113282. **Page 38:** © Bettmann/CORBIS. **Page 39:** © Library of Congress, Prints and Photographs Division, LC-USZ62-128899. **Page 40:** © AP. **Page 41:** © Library of Congress, Prints and Photographs Division, LC-USZ62-115789. **Page 44:** © CP. **Page 45:** © AP.

www.ingramcontent.com/pod-product-compliance
Lightning Source LLC
LaVergne TN
LVHW061332060426
835512LV00013B/2618